BOXERS

KATIE LAJINESS

Big Buddy Books
An Imprint of Abdo Publishing
abdopublishing.com

BIG BUDDY DOGS

abdopublishing.com

Published by Abdo Publishing, a division of ABDO, PO Box 398166, Minneapolis, Minnesota 55439.
Copyright © 2018 by Abdo Consulting Group, Inc. International copyrights reserved in all countries.
No part of this book may be reproduced in any form without written permission from the publisher.
Big Buddy Books™ is a trademark and logo of Abdo Publishing.

Printed in the United States of America, North Mankato, Minnesota.
092017
012018

THIS BOOK CONTAINS
RECYCLED MATERIALS

Cover Photo: Getty Images.
Interior Photos: Drew Angerer/Getty Images (p. 5); Getty Images (pp. 7, 9, 11, 13, 15, 17, 19, 21, 23, 25, 27, 29, 30).

Coordinating Series Editor: Tamara L. Britton
Contributing Editor: Jill Roesler
Graphic Design: Jenny Christensen

Publisher's Cataloging-in-Publication Data

Names: Lajiness, Katie, author.
Title: Boxers / by Katie Lajiness.
Description: Minneapolis, Minnesota : Abdo Publishing, 2018. | Series: Big buddy dogs |
    Includes online resources and index.
Identifiers: LCCN 2017943926 | ISBN 9781532112058 (lib.bdg.) | ISBN 9781614799122 (ebook)
Subjects: LCSH: Boxer (Dog breed)--Juvenile literature. | Dogs--Juvenile literature.
Classification: DDC 636.73--dc23
LC record available at https://lccn.loc.gov/2017943926

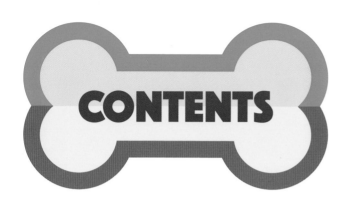

CONTENTS

A POPULAR BREED

Dogs are popular pets. Today, Americans own more than 78 million! Around the world, there are more than 400 dog **breeds**. One of these is the boxer. Let's learn why the boxer is the tenth-most popular breed in the United States.

A boxer claimed the first-place Working Group prize at the 2017 Westminster Kennel Club Dog Show.

THE DOG FAMILY

Dogs come in all shapes and sizes. Yet all dogs belong to the **Canidae** family. The name comes from the Latin word for dog, which is *canis*. This family includes coyotes, foxes, wolves, and more.

Humans and dogs have lived together for at least 16,000 years. In the beginning, humans **bred** them to hunt. Soon, they trained dogs to do other jobs such as guarding property and herding livestock.

Boxers came from a breed of dog called the bullenbeisser (*shown*). Sadly, the bullenbeisser no longer exists.

BOXERS

The boxer comes from a long line of dogs dating back to the 1500s. Its **ancestors** were fighting dogs from the valleys of Tibet.

The boxer **breed** came from Germany during the 1800s. Humans wanted to create a dog that could help hunt large animals. So, when bulldogs, Great Danes, and terriers were mixed, the boxer was born.

The boxer has strong front paws. Some say this breed appears to be boxing when it is fighting or playing.

The boxer became one of the first **breeds** to train as police dogs. Its courage and strength made it the perfect guard dog.

The **American Kennel Club (AKC)** officially recognized the boxer in 1904. During **World War I** and **World War II**, boxers helped protect the soldiers. Today, some boxers work as police or Seeing Eye dogs.

Did you know?

The AKC includes the boxer in the Working Group. These dogs perform jobs such as guarding property and rescuing people.

Boxers are protective of their families. That is what makes them great guard dogs.

WHAT THEY'RE LIKE

Today, the boxer is one of America's favorite dog **breeds**. Boxers are friendly and loyal. A smart breed, they make excellent pets and watchdogs.

Boxers take their watchdog jobs seriously. Sometimes, they can even be cautious around new people. So boxers need an owner who will introduce them to new people and animals.

As both playful and protective pets, boxers make great family dogs.

COAT AND COLOR

Boxers have smooth, short-haired coats. Their coats often have **brindle** or **fawn** coloring. Some have white markings. The **breed** usually has black around its **muzzle** and eyes.

Did you know?

A boxer's fur does not keep it warm in cold weather. A sweater will keep the dog warm when it goes outside in the winter.

About 25 percent of boxers have some white on their coats.

SIZE

Did you know?
A boxer's short mouth and nose cause it to snore!

Boxers are sturdy dogs with long legs and deep chests. Some boxers have **docked** tails. But this practice is against the law in some countries.

These are medium-sized dogs. The males weigh 65 to 80 pounds (29 to 36 kg). They stand 23 to 25 inches (53 to 64 cm) tall. The females are somewhat smaller.

A boxer holds the world record for having the longest canine tongue. It is 17 inches (43 cm) long!

FEEDING

All dogs need food and water to supply energy. Quality dog food provides important **nutrients**. Dogs can eat moist, semimoist, and dry foods. Puppies eat three or more small meals a day. Adult dogs eat one to two times a day.

All dogs need fresh water every day. A healthy 50-pound (23 kg) dog drinks about five cups (1 L) of water a day.

CARE

Boxers require a lot of care. They need regular brushing to keep their coats healthy. Sometimes, they need a bath to help keep them clean. A dog should have its nails trimmed once a month. It should also have its ears checked to avoid **infection**.

Did you know?

Like people, dogs need to have their teeth brushed. Vets suggest brushing your dog's teeth every day.

20

Do not bathe a dog using shampoo for humans. It can make the dog's skin itch.

All dogs need a good veterinarian. The vet can provide health exams and **vaccines** for a boxer. He or she can also **spay** or **neuter** the dog.

Puppies will need to see the vet several times during their first few months. Adult dogs should visit the vet once a year for a checkup.

Take care when traveling with a boxer. As of 2011, snub-nosed breeds cannot be on board an airplane. They have trouble breathing on airplanes.

Daily walks are important. Every dog needs a collar with identification tags. A **microchip** can also keep a boxer safe. This way, an owner can find the pet if it gets lost.

At home, a crate offers a boxer a place to rest. It can also help with housebreaking puppies.

Toys are a great way to help a boxer exercise. Boxers love to play fetch!

PUPPIES

A boxer mother is **pregnant** for about 63 days. Then, she gives birth to a **litter** of about six puppies. All puppies are born blind and deaf. After two weeks, they can see and hear. At three weeks, the puppies begin taking their first steps.

It takes almost three years for a boxer puppy to reach its full size.

THINGS THEY NEED

At eight to 12 weeks old, boxer puppies are ready for **adoption**. When a puppy comes home, the owner should begin obedience training as soon as it is settled.

Boxer puppies like to be active. So, they need daily exercise and training. A boxer will be a loving companion for ten to 12 years.

Teaching a puppy to sit is a basic skill covered in an obedience class.

GLOSSARY

adoption the process of taking responsibility for a pet.

American Kennel Club (AKC) an organization that studies and promotes interest in purebred dogs.

ancestor a family member from an earlier time.

breed a group of animals sharing the same appearance and features. To breed is to produce animals by mating.

brindle having dark streaks or spots on a gray or brownish background.

Canidae (KAN-uh-dee) the scientific Latin name for the dog family. Members of this family are called canids. They include wolves, jackals, foxes, coyotes, and domestic dogs.

dock to cut short, especially a tail or ears.

fawn a light grayish brown.

infection (ihn-FEHK-shun) the causing of an unhealthy condition by something harmful, such as bacteria.

litter all of the puppies born at one time to a mother dog.

microchip an electronic circuit placed under an animal's skin. A microchip contains identifying information that can be read by a scanner.

muzzle an animal's nose and jaws.

neuter (NOO-tuhr) to remove a male animal's reproductive glands.

nutrient (NOO-tree-uhnt) something found in food that living beings take in to live and grow.

pregnant having one or more babies growing within the body.

spay to remove a female animal's reproductive organs.

vaccine (vak-SEEN) a shot given to prevent illness or disease.

World War I a war fought in Europe from 1914 to 1918.

World War II a war fought in Europe, Asia, and Africa from 1939 to 1945.

ONLINE RESOURCES

Booklinks
NONFICTION NETWORK
FREE! ONLINE NONFICTION RESOURCES

To learn more about boxers, visit **abdobooklinks.com**. These links are routinely monitored and updated to provide the most current information available.

INDEX